THE UNIVERSITY OF CHICAGO

CROWN FAMILY SCHOOL OF SOCIAL WORK, POLICY, AND PRACTICE
Advancing a More Just and Humane Society

UCHIC

RESEARCH REPORT   NOVEMBER 2024

English Learners in Chicago Public Schools

A Spotlight on High School Students

Marisa de la Torre, Alyssa Blanchard, Kaitlyn Franklin, Carlos Angeles, & Elaine M. Allensworth

TABLE OF CONTENTS

ACKNOWLEDGEMENTS

The authors would like to acknowledge the many people who contributed to this study, from the early stages to the final publication. Thank you to the Latino Policy Forum (the Forum) for their collaboration and contribution to this line of work. Without their commitment and leadership in convening an advisory committee of experts, this research would not have been possible. A special thanks to Rebecca Vonderlack-Navarro, PhD, Vice President of Education Policy & Research at the Forum, who has been a tireless champion of this project. Prior to writing this report, we presented preliminary findings to the members of our Steering Committee and to the advisory committee convened by the Forum. The advisory committee included Karime Asaf, Peter Auffant, Olimpia Bahena, Stephanie Banchero, Dr. Meg Bates, Patricia Brekke, Hilda Calderón-Peña, Joann Clyde, Andrea Cortés, Chibuzo Ezeigbo, Jane Fleming, Alaynah Garibay, Rosario Hernandez, Christina Herzog, Helyn Kim, Priya Linson, Gudelia López, Jorge Macías, Dominique Mckoy, Destiny Ortega, Sylvia Puente, Miguel Saucedo, Anna Szuber, Allison Tingwall, Ricardo Trujillo, Tomas Uriostegui, Rebecca Vonderlack-Navarro, and Josie Yanguas.

We also thank our colleagues at the UChicago Consortium, including Chen An, Bronwyn McDaniel, Jenny Nagaoka, Jessica Tansey, and Alex Usher who provided helpful feedback at all stages of this report. We are grateful to Lynn Cherkasky-Davis and Mariana Baragán Torres, Steering Committee members, for their thoughtful and careful review. Thanks to Jessica Puller for her careful editing of the manuscript. We also thank our colleague Luvuyo Magwaza who conducted a thorough technical read of the report. Bronwyn McDaniel was instrumental in shepherding this brief through the publication process.

This work was generously funded by the Joyce Foundation and the Crown Family Philanthropies. We also had support from the Institute of Education Sciences, U.S. Department of Education, through Grant R305A220430 to the University of Chicago. The opinions expressed are those of the authors and do not represent views of the Institute or the U.S. Department of Education.

We thank the Consortium Investor Council that funds critical work at the Consortium: putting the research to work, refreshing the data archive, seeding new studies, replicating previous studies, and making research equitable. Members include: Brinson Foundation, CME Group Foundation, Crown Family Philanthropies, Lewis-Sebring Family Foundation, Lloyd A. Fry Foundation, Joyce Foundation, Mayer & Morris Kaplan Family Foundation, McDougal Family Foundation, Robert R. McCormick Foundation, Polk Bros. Foundation, Spencer Foundation, Steans Family Foundation, Square One Foundation, The Chicago Public Education Fund, the Vivo Foundation, and two anonymous foundations. The Consortium also gratefully acknowledges the Lewis-Sebring Family Foundation, whose operating grant supports the work of the UChicago Consortium.

Cite as: de la Torre, M., Blanchard, A., Franklin, K., Angeles, C., & Allensworth, E.M. (2024). *English Learners in Chicago Public Schools: A Spotlight on High School Students.* Chicago, IL: University of Chicago Consortium on School Research.

This report was produced by the UChicago Consortium's publications and communications staff: Jessica Tansey, Managing Director of Communications; Bronwyn McDaniel, Communications Manager, and Jessica Puller, Senior Communications Strategist.

Graphic Design: Jeff Hall Design
Photography: Eileen Ryan, Cynthia Howe
Editing: Bronwyn McDaniel and Jessica Puller

11.2024/PDF/jh.design@rcn.com

Executive Summary

The focus of this study is on understanding different indicators of academic performance in high school, college enrollment, and college persistence of English Learners—including variation in attainment among active and former English Learners—to support their path to high school graduation and access to college.

Recent data from Chicago Public Schools (CPS) show that active English Learners were less likely to graduate from high school (77% did so in 2023) than their peers (85%) and less likely to enroll in college (56% of 2022 English Learners high school graduates enrolled in college compared to 66 percent of their non-English Learners high school graduate peers), drawing attention to what supports these students need and what barriers they face on the road to college.[1]

But publicly reported statistics on English Learners are typically about active English Learners as a whole, and this obscures the possible variability in the skills and needs that English Learners bring with them to high school. In addition, there is a lack of information nationally on how former English Learners (those who were English Learners prior to entering high school) perform in high school and beyond, as districts do not report outcome data for these students separately.

To understand the academic performance in high school, college enrollment, and college persistence of English Learners, this study highlights these metrics for former English Learners and different groups of active English Learners (at the time of enrollment in ninth grade). Active English Learners are divided into

long-term English Learners (English Learners who have been classified as such for six or more years) with and without individualized education plans (IEPs) and late-arriving English Learners (English Learners who have been classified as such for fewer than six years). We make the distinction between these groups because the different experiences and needs of these subgroups are often not recognized. We report Freshman OnTrack rates, cumulative high school GPAs, SAT scores, four-year high school graduation rates, immediate college enrollment rates, and two-year college persistence rates for these groups of students and how their outcomes compared to the district average.

Using three cohorts of students who were first-time ninth-graders in the fall of 2014, 2015, and 2016 where 33% of students were English Learners, we conclude that English Learners are not perpetually struggling, as publicly reported numbers suggest, but specific groups of English Learners need more support. There are some commonalities among English Learners, but also some key differences, suggesting that there are different strategies that would be effective in supporting different English Learners groups. In particular, we have learned:

---

1 Chicago Public Schools (2024a).

- **Former English Learners**, students who were *formerly* classified as English Learners during their time in CPS but demonstrated English proficiency and exited English Learner (EL) status by the ninth grade, represented 23% of the ninth-grade student population and the majority of students ever classified as English Learners in these three cohorts.

  - They had academic achievement (cumulative GPAs and SAT scores) and attainment (high school graduation and college enrollment rates), including two-year persistence in college among college enrollees, higher than the district average.

  - Their two-year college enrollment rate was higher than the district average, while their four-year college enrollment rate was similar to the district average.

Former English Learners were academically strong students in high school and were able to persist in college in large numbers. Many of them enrolled in two-year colleges right after high school. There is a need to understand how the choices these students are making to go to two-year colleges instead of four-year colleges influence their long-term educational attainment and careers. Two-year colleges provide a low-cost and local opportunity for college. But at the same time, completion rates are lower in two-year colleges than four-year colleges.

- **Long-term English Learners without IEPs**, *active English Learners* in the ninth grade who had been in CPS for six or more years (i.e., third grade or earlier) without demonstrating English proficiency through the ACCESS test and *did not* have an IEP for an *identified disability* at the beginning of ninth grade, represented 4% of the ninth-grade student population.

  - Their academic achievement (cumulative GPA and SAT scores) and attainment throughout high school and post-secondary years was substantially lower than the district average.

  - They were more likely to enroll in two-year colleges and less likely to enroll in four-year colleges than the district average.

  - Among students who enrolled in four-year colleges, they had lower persistence rates than their peers.

Long-term English Learners without IEPs need help transitioning to high school in addition to more support throughout high school. They were less likely to be on-track in ninth grade than any other group, which means they failed some of their classes and seemed less likely to get support in ninth grade than other students. For those enrolling in four-year colleges, they may need more support to get a degree as their persistence rate was lower than their peers. Their needs may not be recognized when reporting is done for all active English Learners.

- **Long-term English Learners with IEPs**, *active English Learners* in the ninth grade who had been in CPS for *six or more years* (i.e., third grade or earlier) without demonstrating English proficiency through the ACCESS test and had an IEP for an *identified disability* at the beginning of ninth grade, represented 3% of the ninth-grade student population.

  - These students' outcomes were below the district average, except for Freshman OnTrack, but they had similar performance and attainment compared to other students with IEPs.

  - Their college enrollment patterns, enrollment rates, and persistence rates were also similar to non-English Learners with IEPs.

Long-term English Learners with IEPs had similar struggles as other students with IEPs. They seemed to get sufficient support in ninth grade, but then fell behind in the following years. This suggests the need for more support for all students with IEPs that continues through all four years of high school. They are also likely to need special support for choosing colleges that have strong resources for students with disabilities, because they are more likely to struggle in college than other students.

- **Late-arriving English Learners**, *active English Learners* in the ninth grade who had been in CPS for *fewer than six years* (i.e., after third grade), represented 3% of the ninth-grade student population.

  - They were less likely to be Latinx than other English Learners groups (57% Latinx students for this group vs. around 90% Latinx for other English Learners).

- Their high school graduation was 81%, very close to the district average of 84%, but their SAT scores were low.
- They were more likely to enroll in a two-year college and less likely to enroll in a four-year college, when compared to the district average. And their two-year college persistence was higher than most other students who enrolled in college.

Late-arriving English Learners struggled with standardized tests in English as they were still learning English while in high school, but their grades were as strong as, or stronger than, other students and they were just as likely to graduate from high school. They were more successful than never English Learners and former English Learners when they got to college, suggesting that their low-test scores were not indicative of a lower likelihood of success. They may need more support around the college enrollment process—they were underrepresented in four-year colleges and overrepresented in two-year colleges, despite having strong high school GPAs.

Continuously reporting only on active English Learners and the gaps in scores on tests given in English obscures the successes of English Learners as a group. At the same time, not recognizing the heterogeneity in this group does not allow us to identify that specific groups of English Learners need more support. This study shines a light on what those areas of need are.

CHAPTER 1

Introduction

The focus of this study is on understanding different indicators of academic performance in high school, college enrollment, and college persistence of English Learners in order to support their path to high school graduation and access to college.

English Learners in high school are a particular group of students who need attention, as the academic demands are higher while they are trying to acquire the academic English skills that will allow them to fully participate in English-based classes. Each class has content-specific vocabulary, and reading and writing skills become more complex with a more limited time to acquire them than in earlier grades. Recent data from Chicago Public Schools (CPS) show that active English Learners were less likely to graduate from high school (77% did so in 2023) than their peers (85%).[2] Among those who graduated from high school, the differences in the likelihood of enrolling in college was even larger (56 % of 2022 English Learners high school graduates enrolled in college, compared to 66 percent of their non-English Learners high school graduate peers), drawing attention to what supports these students need and what barriers they face on the road to college.[3]

Publicly reported statistics on English Learners are typically about active English Learners as a whole, and this obscures the possible variability in the skills and needs that English Learners bring with them to high school. Some students might have been classified as English Learners for a long time, with levels of academic English proficiency that do not allow them to make

a transition toward reclassification but strong social English language skills. Other English Learners might be more recent arrivals to U.S. schools with no, low, or modest levels of English language skills. Some of them might have interrupted schooling, but some might be academically advanced.

Furthermore, there is a lack of information nationally on how former English Learners (those who were English Learners prior to entering high school) perform in high school and beyond, as districts do not report outcome data for these students separately. Prior research from Chicago shows that former English Learners are strong academically—often outperforming students never classified as English Learners.[4] However, English Learners' access to rigorous academic content in school is an issue, as they are less likely to be enrolled than non-English Learner students in upper-level classes that would prepare them for college-level work.[5]

This lack of information on high school English Learners' performance, given their diverse academic and linguistic skills, motivates our research question:

- *What is the academic performance in high school, college enrollment, and college persistence of former English Learners (students once classified as English Learners but who have demonstrated proficiency) and*

---

2 Chicago Public Schools (2024a).
3 Chicago Public Schools (2024b).
4 de la Torre, Blanchard, Allensworth, & Freire (2019).
5 Umansky (2016); Olsen (2010).

different groups of active English Learners (long-term English Learners, with and without individualized education plans (IEPs), and late-arriving English Learners) compared to the district average?

Answering this question is a starting point to understand how to support all English Learners in high school and beyond.

Using three cohorts of recent high school students in CPS, we found that active English Learners in high school were a very diverse group of students with different outcomes. Those classified as long-term English Learners had more difficulty in high school, were less likely to enroll in college, and were less likely to persist if they did enroll in college. All English Learners, including former English Learners who performed well in high school, were more likely to enroll in two-year colleges compared to the district average. These results imply that active English Learners need different supports as they face different challenges in high school, and that all English Learners face barriers to accessing four-year colleges, compared to native English language students.

CHAPTER 2

Study Details

Analytic Sample

The study focuses on three cohorts of students—those who started ninth grade for the first time in the fall of 2014, 2015, and 2016; a total of 78,507 students—and their later outcomes.[6] The outcomes of interest in this study are: Freshman OnTrack status, four-year high school graduation rates, cumulative high school GPA until time of graduation, SAT scores in eleventh grade among high school graduates, immediate college enrollment rates in any college, two-year and four-year college enrollment among college enrollees, and two-year college persistence rates among enrollees in two-year and four-year colleges (see the Appendix for definitions).[7]

Classification of English Learners

A student was classified as an English learner if 1) when they enrolled in CPS, a parent or guardian indicated that a language other than English was spoken by the student or at home, and 2) a screener assessment for English proficiency indicated that the student was not at the level necessary to fully participate in an English-based classroom. Every year *active English Learners* take the ACCESS test of English proficiency. If they score at or above a certain cut-off that determines their English skills, they exit EL classification and become *former English Learners.*[8]

The classification as an English Learner for the students in the study was based on their status at the beginning of ninth grade. In our sample, 23% of the ninth-grade students were former English Learners and 10% were active English Learners (see Figure 1). We divided the active English Learners into three subgroups: 1) long-term English Learners without Individualized Education Plans (IEPs), 2) long-term English Learners with IEPs, and 3) late-arriving English Learners.[9]

The definitions of these groups are as follows:

- **Former English Learners:** Students who were *formerly* classified as English Learners during their time in CPS but demonstrated English proficiency and exited EL status by the ninth grade.

- **Long-term English Learners without an IEP:** *Active English Learners* in the ninth grade who had been in CPS for *six or more years* (i.e., third grade or earlier) without demonstrating English proficiency through the ACCESS test and *did not* have an IEP for an *identified disability* at the beginning of ninth grade.[10] This group was the largest among active English Learners and accounted for 4% of first-time ninth-graders in the sample.

- **Long-term English Learners with an IEP:** *Active English Learners* in the ninth grade who had been in CPS for *six or more years* (i.e., third grade or earlier) without demonstrating English proficiency through the ACCESS test and had an IEP for an *identified*

---

6 Students were not part of the analytic sample if they enrolled for fewer than 110 days during their ninth-grade year or if their attendance data was not available for that year. This ensures that students were enrolled in CPS schools long enough to take the ACCESS test, which is typically given in January. This test is required for students classified as English Learners and it helps us define who is classified as an English Learner.

7 Another important milestone is college completion; however, we would need a few more years to pass to report this outcome given that some of these students are probably still pursuing their post-graduate degree. Future studies will include college completion.

8 The ACCESS test is the assessment that tests English proficiency skills for students from K through twelfth grade.

9 Students with an IEP require special education instruction, supports, and services that students with disabilities are legally required to receive. An IEP is developed by school staff members, the student's parents/guardians, and the students (when appropriate).

10 A small group of these students, 2%, was identified with a disability during the high school years but continued to be classified in the group without an IEP as we classified students based on their status in ninth grade.

disability at the beginning of ninth grade.[11] This group accounted for 3% of first-time ninth-graders in the sample, the second largest among active English Learners.

- **Late-arriving English Learners:** *Active English Learners* in the ninth grade who had been in CPS for *fewer than six years* (i.e., after third grade). These students could be more likely to be born outside of the United States, to have schooling in another country, or to be classified as refugees. Late-arriving English Learners accounted for 3% of first-time ninth-graders in the sample.[12]

The rest of the students, who have never been classified as English Learners, will be referred to as *never English Learners* and represented two-thirds of the first-time ninth-graders in our cohorts.

Student Characteristics

Tables 1 and 2 provide a descriptive overview of the sample detailing key characteristics of English Learners in CPS who were part of the study. These are some of the main characteristics of the different groups:

- **Former English Learners,** compared to never English Learners, were:
  - more likely to be free or reduced-price lunch eligible and Latinx,

- less likely to have an IEP, and
- less likely to transfer out of CPS during high school.

- **Long-term English Learners with and without IEPs** were:
  - almost all free or reduced-price lunch (FRPL) eligible and Latinx, and
  - long-term English Learners with IEPs were more likely to be male than students in any other group.

    - When long-term English Learners with IEP were compared to non-English Learners with IEPs, they (**see Table 2**):
      - were more likely to be identified with a learning disability and less likely to be identified with a behavioral one,
      - had similar representation of male students, and
      - were more likely to be free or reduced-price lunch (FRPL) eligible.

- **Late-Arriving English Learners:**
  - were less likely to be Latinx than other English Learners,
  - close to one-third newly enrolled in ninth grade, and
  - were more likely to transfer out of CPS than other students.

FIGURE 1

At the beginning of high school, one-third of students were active or former English Learners

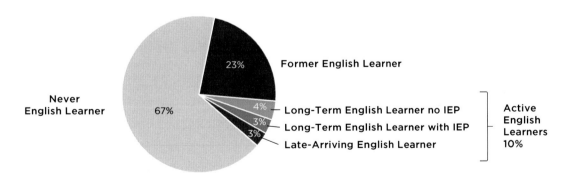

Note: There are 78,507 students represented in this figure. They entered ninth grade for the first time in the fall of 2014, 2015, and 2016.

---

11 If a student had an IEP labeled as "504" (students with physical disabilities who do not receive special education services), we do not consider them students with an identified disability, and they are excluded from this category.

12 Combining all groups of English learner students into a single "ever English Learners" category can reveal meaningful information about the overall journey of English Learners. And although it is not the main focus of this study, we provide that information on p.20 in a box entitled "Ever vs. Never English Learners."

TABLE 1

Characteristics of the students in the study

	All	Never English Learners	Former English Learners	Active English Learners		
				Long-term English Learners no IEP	Long-term English Learners with IEP	Late-arriving English Learners
Number	78,507	52,468	18,089	3,012	2,648	2,290
Male	50%	49%	50%	52%	65%	54%
Free or Reduced-Price Lunch (FRPL) **Eligible**	84%	79%	93%	97%	96%	80%
Race						
Latinx	47%	28%	86%	94%	93%	57%
Black	39%	57%	1%	2%	1%	7%
White	8%	10%	6%	2%	3%	11%
Asian/Pacific Islander	4%	2%	6%	2%	2%	20%
Other	2%	3%	<1%	<1%	<1%	5%
Individualized Education Plan (IEP)*	15%	15%	5%	0%	100%	6%
Learning Disability	10%	10%	4%	0%	77%	4%
Cognitive Disability	2%	3%	<1%	0%	16%	1%
Physical Disability	1%	2%	1%	0%	5%	1%
Behavioral Disability	1%	1%	<1%	0%	2%	<1%
Speech and Language Disability	<1%	<1%	<1%	0%	<1%	<1%
New to CPS in ninth grade	4%	5%	0%	0%	0%	29%
Transferred out of CPS after ninth grade	9%	10%	6%	8%	7%	18%

Note: *We present five different categories of disability in this table among the 14 categories of disability present in CPS administrative data. These five are: learning disability (disabilities that affect how the brain processes information, such as dyslexia), cognitive disability (disabilities affecting mental processes, such as autism), physical disability (disabilities with a limitation on the physical functioning, mobility, dexterity, or stamina), behavioral disability (disabilities that involve a pattern of disruptive behaviors), and speech and language disability (communication disorders that adversely affects a child's educational performance, such as impaired articulation).

TABLE 2
Characteristics of students in the study with IEPs

	Long-term English Learners with IEP	Never English Learners with IEP
Number	2,648	8,037
Male	65%	64%
Free or Reduced-Price Lunch (FRPL) **Eligible**	96%	88%
Race		
Latinx	93%	22%
Black	1%	68%
White	3%	8%
Asian/Pacific Islander	2%	<1%
Other	<1%	1%
Individualized Education Plan (IEP)	100%	100%
Learning Disability	77%	65%
Cognitive Disability	16%	17%
Physical Disability	5%	10%
Behavioral Disability	2%	7%
Speech and Language Disability	<1%	1%
New to CPS in ninth grade	0%	<1%
Transferred out of CPS after ninth grade	7%	12%

Methods

We used descriptive statistics and regression models for this study. All figures illustrate descriptive statistics. Because student characteristics are different across the groups as described above, we ran regression models that take those characteristics into account to determine whether *comparing students who are similar in those dimensions* would give us more insights into the findings. The results of regression models are discussed in the text if they provide different conclusions than the simple comparisons of the descriptive results shown in figures (see the Appendix for the estimates from regression models).

Describing the Differences in Outcomes

Methodology

In general, researchers describe whether differences in outcomes are important based on statistical tests (guided by p-values or statistical significance to determine whether differences are different from zero) or by their size, categorizing them as small, medium, or large compared to the standard deviation of the outcome (a measure of the variation observed) or compared to other known gaps as income or race gaps.[A]

Given the large number of students in our study, many of the differences are statistically significant (see the tables in the Appendix), so we will guide our description of whether gaps are substantially different or meaningful by the gap size (measured in standard deviation units). We describe outcomes as being substantially or meaningfully different among groups of students when the difference is 0.2 standard deviations or higher, otherwise we will describe the differences as higher or lower but not considerably different, even when they are statistically different.

While there is no clear consensus among researchers on how to classify the size of differences in education, we think that a 0.2 standard deviations gap is substantial enough to highlight so groups of students can be prioritized for supports when the differences are of this magnitude. Table A contains the standard deviation and the value of the 0.2 standard deviation for each of the outcomes in the study. For example, among the students in the study sample, the standard deviation for cumulative high school GPA was 0.72 points, thus a 0.2 standard deviation was 0.14 points. If the GPA difference between two groups of students was larger than 0.14, it will be reported in the text that their GPAs are meaningfully different.

In addition, the last column in Table A presents the value of the difference between free or reduced-price lunch eligible and ineligible students as a point of reference of how large or small those are, as socioeconomic status is a strongly correlated with educational outcomes.[B]

TABLE A

Outcome distributions and gaps

	Standard deviation based on study sample	0.2 standard deviation	Free or Reduced-Price Lunch Eligible Gap (in absolute value)
Freshman OnTrack rate	33 percentage points (pp)	7 pp	9 pp
Four-year graduation rate	37 pp	7 pp	11 pp
Cumulative high school GPA	0.72	0.14	0.48
SAT scores	190	38	181
Immediate college enrollment			
Overall	46 pp	9 pp	17 pp
Two-year college enrollment	46 pp	9 pp	7 pp*
Four-year college enrollment	46 pp	9 pp	24pp
Two-year college persistence			
Among two-year college enrollees	50 pp	10 pp	17 pp
Among four-year college enrollees	46 pp	9 pp	19 pp

Note: *Free or reduced-price eligible students were more likely to enroll in two-year colleges, hence this gap goes in the opposite direction from all other gaps described in the table where free or reduced-price eligible students had lower outcomes than their peers.

A   Cohen (1988).
B   Rouse (2007).

CHAPTER 3

Findings

HIGH SCHOOL MILESTONES

Freshman OnTrack and Four-Year High School Graduation

High school graduation is a crucial milestone for an individual, setting a foundation for future success. Research has shown that high school graduates have lower unemployment rates and higher earnings, are less likely to engage in criminal activities, have better health outcomes, and have a higher life expectancy than high school dropouts.[13] Freshman OnTrack is an early warning indicator of whether students are on-track to graduate from high school, helping identify students who may be at risk of not graduating on time. Research indicates that students who are on-track at the end of their ninth-grade year, defined as earning enough credits to advance to tenth grade and not failing more than one semester core course, are significantly more likely to graduate high school when compared to their peers who are not on-track.[14]

Findings

Freshman OnTrack rates and four-year graduation rates were not substantially different from the district average for former English Learners **and** late-arriving English Learners.

- **Former English Learners** had the highest Freshman OnTrack and graduation rates, 90% and 88% respectively **(see Figures 2 and 3)**, while the district averages were 88% and 84% respectively.

- **Late-arriving English Learners** had a Freshman OnTrack rate of 87% and a graduation rate of 81%.

  - Despite joining U.S. schools later in their schooling, most late-arriving English Learners were able to pass their classes and accumulate enough credits throughout their high school career to graduate in four years.

Long-term English Learners **had substantially lower four-year graduation rates than their peers.**

- **Long-term English Learners without IEPs** had the lowest Freshman OnTrack rate (77%), suggesting that this group was having a hard time passing their classes and earning credits in ninth grade, compared to other students. Their graduation rate was 74% which, although not the lowest among their peers, was 10 percentage points lower than the district average.

- **Long-term English Learners with IEPs** had a Freshman OnTrack rate similar to the district average (86%). However, this did not translate to a graduation rate (69%) similar to the district average.

  - The pattern of a high Freshman OnTrack rate but low graduation rate was similar to non-English Learners with IEPs, who had a Freshman OnTrack rate of 84% and a graduation rate of 70%, pointing to similar performance compared to other students with IEPs.[15]

  - While long-term English Learners with IEPs did well in their first year of high school, their performance in subsequent years did not allow many of them to graduate from high school within four years. When calculating six-year graduation rates to allow for two more years to fulfill the graduation requirements, we found that 77% of long-term English Learners with IEPs graduated. This rate is still substantially lower than the six-year district average (89%) and similar to other students with an IEP (79%).

---

13 Rouse (2007); Moretti (2007); Cutler & Lleras-Muney (2006).
14 Allensworth & Easton (2005).
15 See also Table A.2 in the Appendix that shows that when long-term English Learners with IEPs were compared to similar students with IEPs their high school graduation rates were not substantially different (under 0.2 standard deviations).

16 Bowen, Chingos, & McPherson (2009); Allensworth, & Clark (2020); Roderick, Nagaoka, Allensworth, Coca, Correa, & Stoker (2006); Healey, Nagaoka, & Michelman (2014).

FIGURE 2

Most students' Freshman OnTrack rates were similar, except for long-term English Learners without IEPs

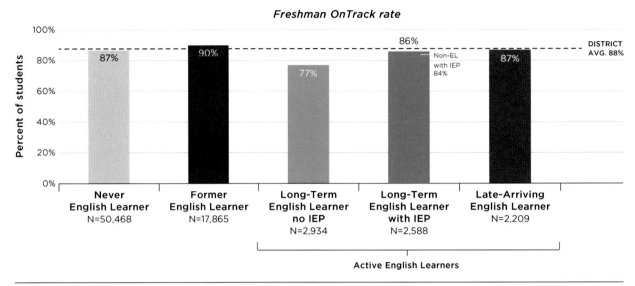

Freshman OnTrack rate

Note: A student is on-track if they fail no more than one semester of a core course and earns at least five credits by the end of their ninth-grade year. The students represented in this graph are students who entered ninth grade for the first time in the fall of 2014, 2015, and 2016 and had non-missing on-track data. The standard deviation for this outcome in our sample is 33 percentage points. An appreciable difference of 0.2 standard deviations is equivalent to 7 percentage points.

FIGURE 3

Long-term English Learners had substantially lower high school graduation rates than their peers

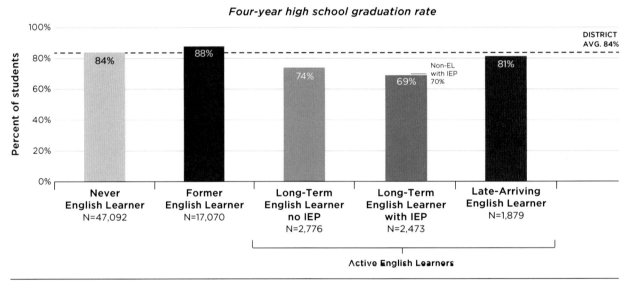

Four-year high school graduation rate

Note: The students represented in this graph are students who entered ninth grade for the first time in the fall of 2014, 2015, and 2016 and did not transfer out of CPS in the four years since enrolling in ninth grade. The standard deviation for this outcome in our sample is 37 percentage points. An appreciable difference of 0.2 standard deviations is equivalent to 7 percentage points.

Cumulative high school GPA and SAT scores

Prior research shows that cumulative high school GPA and standardized assessment scores (i.e., the SAT or ACT) are the academic qualifications most related to college enrollment and success. SAT scores and GPA are related to college access, while GPA is particularly predictive of college success. A GPA of 3.0 or higher is associated with at least a 50% probability of graduating from college among students who enroll in a four-year college.[16]

Findings

The cumulative GPA and SAT scores of former English Learners who graduated high school were slightly higher than the district average, but not substantially different.

- The cumulative GPA of former English Learners was 2.90, compared to the district average of 2.81 (see Figure 4).
    - Former English Learners performed well in their classes, with average cumulative GPAs that signal being ready for college work.
- SAT scores followed a similar pattern: former English Learners had slightly higher composite scores (1003 points) than the district average (977 points; see Figure 5).[17]
    - Former English Learners were able to demonstrate their reading and math skills through standardized assessments given in English.

Long-term English Learners had considerably lower cumulative GPA and SAT scores compared to the district average among those who graduated from high school.

- **Long-term English Learners without IEPs** had the lowest cumulative GPA (2.50)
    - Their SAT scores were also considerably lower (838) than the district average.[18]
    - Even though these students graduated from high school, their cumulative GPAs and SAT scores indicated that they had a harder time academically in high school than other students.
    - Prior research indicates that these students were already struggling in earlier grades.[19]

- **Long-term English Learners with IEPs** also had low cumulative GPA (2.55) and the lowest SAT scores (771) among all the groups of students as depicted in Figure 5.[20]
    - However, the outcomes of these students were not very different from non-English Learners who also had IEPs (see Table A.3 in the Appendix). Both English Learners and non-English Learners with IEPs had similar performance when it comes to cumulative GPA and SAT scores, which was well below the district average.

Late-arriving English Learners had slightly higher cumulative GPAs but substantially lower SAT scores, when compared to the district average among those who graduated high school.

- **Late-arriving English Learners** had a 2.87 cumulative GPA—similar to former English Learners, never English Learners, and the district average.
    - Even though their English language skills were not deemed proficient when they started high school, these students were able to meet the expectations of their teachers in high school.
- **Late-arriving English Learners** scored low on the SAT assessments in eleventh grade (882), compared to the district average.[21]
    - Even though their English language knowledge was not a major barrier to demonstrating their skills in the classes they took in high school, standardized tests were more difficult for these students who were still in the process of acquiring academic English skills.[22]

---

17 A different way to compare SAT scores is through the results based on a national sample of students as published by SAT. A composite score of 1000 translates into a 48th percentile in national sample while a score of 980 corresponds to a 44th percentile (College Board, 2023). .

18 A composite score of 840 corresponds to the 20th percentile in a national sample.

19 Olsen (2010); Umansky (2016).

20 A composite score of 770 corresponds to the 10th percentile in a national sample.

FIGURE 4

Long-term English Learners with no IEPs had lower cumulative GPAs

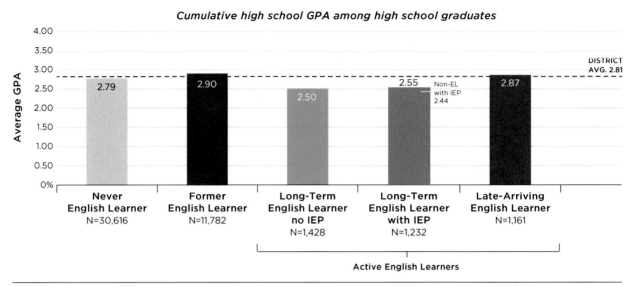

Cumulative high school GPA among high school graduates

Note: Cumulative high school GPA is the average GPA of all the courses a student took from the beginning of high school to the time of graduation. The students represented in this graph are students who entered ninth grade for the first time in the fall of 2014, 2015, and 2016 and graduated high school within four years. Students who attended a charter school are not included in this graph as our data archive currently does not include records of charter school students' course performance. The standard deviation for this outcome in our sample is 0.72 GPA points. An appreciable difference of 0.2 standard deviations is equivalent to 0.14 GPA points.

FIGURE 5

All active English Learners had SAT scores well below the district average

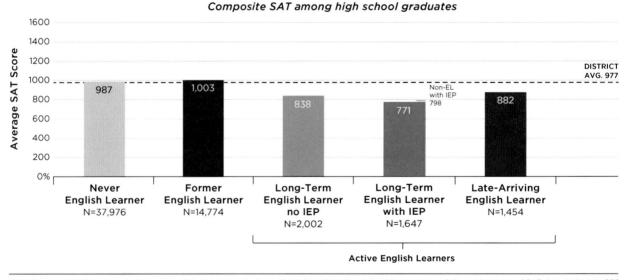

Composite SAT among high school graduates

Note: Composite SAT scores are the average of two assessments, the evidence-based reading and writing section and the math section of SAT that students in CPS take in eleventh grade. The students represented in this graph are students who entered ninth grade for the first time in the fall of 2014, 2015, and 2016 and graduated high school within four years. The standard deviation for this outcome in our sample is 190 points. An appreciable difference of 0.2 standard deviations is equivalent to 38 points.

---

21 A composite score of 880 corresponds to the 26th percentile in a national sample.

22 While English Learners have some testing supports while taking the SAT exams (supports include translated test directions, use of bilingual word-to-word dictionaries, and 50% extended testing time), the evidence-based reading and writing section and the math section of SAT are written in English.

Enrollment: Rates and Patterns

A college degree is increasingly being seen as a necessary step toward securing a well-paying job, and more students are reporting that their educational expectations include a college credential. Among the students in our study, close to 80% reported in ninth grade that they aspired to earn at least a post-secondary degree or certificate.[23] Research shows that students who enroll in college immediately after high school graduation are much more likely to finish college than those who delay enrollment.[24] In addition, enrolling in a four-year institution rather than a two-year one increases the odds that students will persist in college and complete a degree.[25] While immediate college enrollment is highly correlated with college completion, it may not be the best path for everyone. Ultimately, the right choice depends on individual circumstances.

Findings

All English Learners, including former English Learners, were more likely to enroll in a two-year college than the district average.

- While 20% of CPS high school graduates enrolled in a two-year college, English Learners had enrollment rates of 25% or higher (**see Figure 6**).

  - The differences were substantial for **long-term English Learners without IEPs** and **late-arriving English Learners.**

    - When comparing students with similar demographic characteristics, the differences in two-year college enrollment rates diminished for **long-term English Learners without IEPs** (**See regression results in Table A.6 in the Appendix**).

- In general, the gaps diminished for most groups of English Learners, compared to similar students as Latinx students are in general more likely to attend a two-year college and most English Learners were Latinx.

- However, the substantial differences in two-year enrollment rates remained for late-arriving English Learners, when compared to similar students.

Enrollment rates in four-year colleges for former English Learners were similar to the district average.

- Former English Learners had a four-year college enrollment rate just below the district average (45% vs. 46%), while never English Learners had a slightly higher four-year college enrollment rate (49%).

---

23 The data comes from the *5Essentials* Survey that CPS students take every year. Students answer the following question: What is the highest level of education you plan to complete? With possible answers being: **1)** Not planning to complete high school, **2)** High school, **3)** Career/technical school, **4)** 2-year community college or junior college, **5)** 4-year college or university, **6)** Graduate or professional school, **7)** Undecided, or **8)** Other. The response rates for this question were at or above 70% all groups of students (ranging from 70% for long-term English learners with an IEP to 85% for former

English learners). There were differences in these aspirations among groups of students, but all groups of students were more likely than not to aspire to a college degree (82% of never English learners, 81% of former English learners, 67% of long-term English Learners with no IEP, 61% of long-term English Learners with IEP, and 73% of late-arriving English Learners).

24 Healey et al. (2014); Mahaffie, Usher, Nagaoka, & McKoy (2024).

25 Bowen et al. (2009).

All active English Learners, both long-term and late-arriving English Learners, were considerably less likely to enroll in four-year colleges than their peers.

- **Long-term English Learners** had particularly low enrollment numbers, with only 23% of those without IEPs and 17% of those with IEPs enrolling in a four-year college, compared to the district average of 46%.
  - Long-term English Learners had lower cumulative GPA and SAT scores than their peers in high school, which might have contributed to their low enrollment rates in four-year colleges.
  - The college enrollment patterns of **long-term English Learners with IEPs** followed that of non-English Learners with IEPs, who were less likely than the average student to enroll in a four-year college (18%) and more likely to do so in a two-year college (25%), and overall college enrollment was low for students with an IEP.[26]

- **Late-arriving English Learners** enrolled in four-year colleges at a rate of 32%.
  - Although late-arriving English Learners had high cumulative GPAs compared to the district average, their lower performance on standardized tests might have reduced their overall qualifications for college entry—potentially contributing to the lower-than-average enrollment rate.

FIGURE 6

All English Learners, including former English Learners, were more likely to enroll in a two-year college; long-term English Learners had particularly low enrollment in four-year colleges

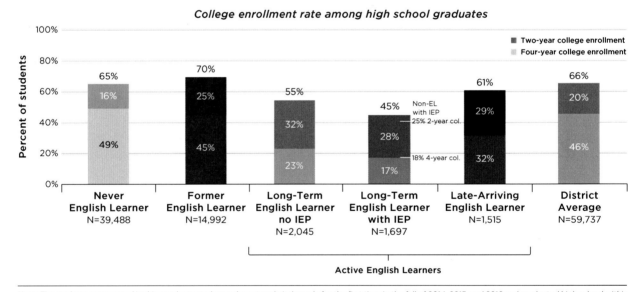

College enrollment rate among high school graduates

Note: The students represented in this graph are students who entered ninth grade for the first time in the fall of 2014, 2015, and 2016 and graduated high school within four years of starting ninth grade. A student is considered a "college enrollee" if they enrolled in a two- or four-year college within those same four years. Students are counted toward the two-year college enrollment rate if they enrolled in a two-year college within those same four years. Students are counted toward the four-year college enrollment rate if they enrolled in a four-year college within those same four years. The standard deviation for all three of these outcomes in our sample is 46 percentage points. An appreciable difference of 0.2 standard deviations is equivalent to 9 percentage points.

26 See also Table A.7 in the Appendix that shows that when long-term English Learners with IEPs were compared to similar students with IEPs their four-year college enrollment rates were not substantially different (under 0.2 standard deviations).

Two-Year College Persistence

Students who enroll in college can find difficulties along the way. Regardless of whether they are enrolled in a two- or four-year college, prior research indicates that students who remain continuously enrolled through the first two years of college are more likely to complete a degree or credential.[27] Students who enroll in two-year colleges can potentially get their degree in this period of time and/or transfer to a four-year college, so either of these scenarios are counted as persistence in our analysis.

Findings

All groups of students who enrolled in two-year colleges had similar two-year persistence compared to the district average, with former English Learners and late-arriving English Learners showing the highest rates.

- 49% of **former English Learners** and 48% of **late-arriving English Learners** persisted in two-year colleges for two years, compared to a district average of 44% (**see Figure 7**).

- Students who attended two-year colleges could potentially earn an associate degree within two years of enrollment. Just 9% among the students who enrolled in two-year colleges in our sample did. This is a much smaller number than students who persisted for two years, suggesting that it might take students longer to get an associate degree or that some students may have transferred to a four-year college.

Former and late-arriving English Learners who enrolled in four-year colleges had high two-year persistence college rates compared to the district average, especially late-arriving English Learners.

- 74% of **former English Learners** persisted in four-year colleges for two years, similar to the district average of 70% (**see Figure 8**).

- **Late-arriving English Learners** had a slightly higher two-year persistence rate in four-year colleges at 78%.

  - While their enrollment in four-year college was below district average (32% vs. 46% for the district average), those who enrolled persisted at higher rates than even former English Learners.

Long-term English Learners who enrolled in four-year colleges were less likely to persist in college than their peers, especially those with IEPs whose rates were substantially lower.

- 63% of **long-term English Learners without IEPs** who enrolled in four-year colleges remained enrolled in college after two years, which was lower than the district average (**see Figure 8**).

- **Long-term English Learners with IEPs** had a two-year persistence rate of 55%, compared to the district average of 70%.

  - While their cumulative GPA was not very different from long-term English Learners without IEPs (2.50 for long-term English Learners without IEPs vs. 2.55 for long-term English Learners with IEPs), students with an identified disability had a more difficult time persisting in college than other long-term English Learners. However, other students with IEPs, who had similar cumulative GPAs, had a similarly low two-year persistence rate of 53%.[28]

---

27 Nagaoka, Lee, Usher, & Seeskin (2021).

28 See also Table A.9 in the Appendix that shows that when long-term English Learners with IEPs were compared to similar students with IEPs their two-year persistence in four-year colleges were not substantially different (under 0.2 standard deviations).

FIGURE 7

English Learners' two-year college persistence was similar to the district average among two-year college enrollees

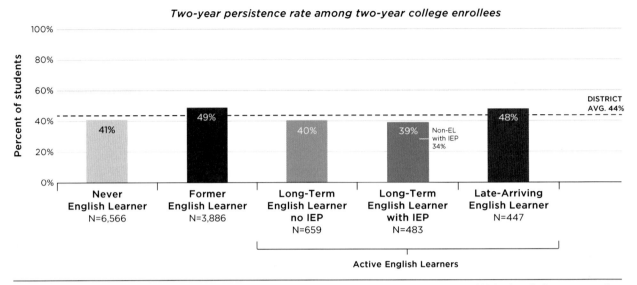

Two-year persistence rate among two-year college enrollees

Note: The students represented in this graph are students who entered ninth grade for the first time in the fall of 2014, 2015, and 2016 and enrolled in a two-year college within four years of starting ninth grade. A student is considered to have persisted in college for two years if they were enrolled in college for at least two years, with records in four consecutive fall and spring terms, or attained an associate degree or bachelor's degree, within six years of starting ninth grade. The standard deviation for this outcome in our sample is 50 percentage points. An appreciable difference of 0.2 standard deviations is equivalent to 10 percentage points.

FIGURE 8

Long-term English Learners with an IEP were less likely to persist in four-year colleges among four-year college enrollees; their rates were similar to non-English Learners with IEPs

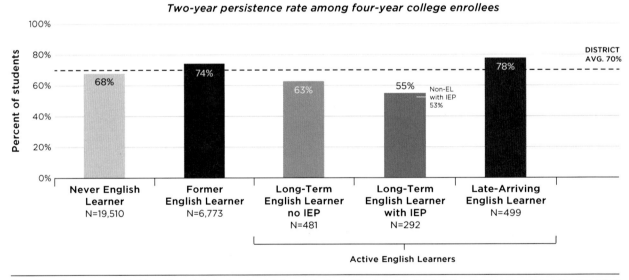

Two-year persistence rate among four-year college enrollees

Note: The students represented in this graph are students who entered ninth grade for the first time in the fall of 2014, 2015, and 2016 and enrolled in a four-year college within four years of starting ninth grade. A student is considered to have persisted in college for two years if they were enrolled in college for at least two years, with records in four consecutive fall and spring terms, or attained an associate degree or bachelor's degree, within six years of starting ninth grade. The standard deviation for this outcome in our sample is 46 percentage points. An appreciable difference of 0.2 standard deviations is equivalent to 9 percentage points.

Combining all groups of English Learners into a single "ever English Learner" category can reveal meaningful information about the overall journey of English Learners

While looking at outcomes by different groups of English Learners can show us areas of success and areas needing support, we also report outcomes for "ever English Learners" to give parents or district decisionmakers an understanding of what to expect when students start their academic journey as an English Learner.

- The attainment of "ever English Learners" represents the average student who begins their time in CPS as an English Learner, and includes former English Learners, long-term English Learners without IEPs, long-term English Learners with IEPs, and late-arriving English Learners in a single category.

Ever English Learners had similar high school outcomes, including cumulative GPA and SAT scores, to students who were never classified as English Learners.

- Ever English Learners were just as likely to be classified as on-track for graduation at the end of their ninth-grade year as never English Learners (88% vs. 87%, **see Figure A**).

- Ever English Learners were equally likely to graduate in four years as never English Learners (84% vs. 84%).

- Among high school graduates, ever English Learners had similar cumulative GPAs (2.83 vs. 2.79) and SAT scores (958 vs. 987) compared to never English Learners.

  - Even though their academic English skills were not deemed proficient when they entered CPS, these students were able to meet the requirements for on-time high school graduation at the same rate as their peers and demonstrate their academic skills in the classroom and in standardized tests.

Ever English Learners' overall college enrollment rate was similar to never English Learners, but they were less likely to enroll in a four-year college and more likely to enroll in a two-year college than never English Learners.

- Ever English Learners high school graduates had lower enrollment rates in four-year colleges than never English Learners (39% vs. 49%).

  - Despite the fact that ever English Learner graduates had similar cumulative GPA and SAT scores to never English Learners, they were less likely to enroll in a four-year college.

- Ever English Learner high school graduates had a higher enrollment rate in two-year colleges than never English Learners (26% vs. 16%).

  - However, 77% of ever English Learners said in the ninth grade that they aspired to earn at least a four-year degree.[C]

    - Immediately enrolling in a two-year college is associated with a lower likelihood of completing a four-year degree than immediately enrolling in a four-year college[D] This means that ever English Learners might not be on the path to earn the four-year degree to which they aspire.

Once ever English Learners were enrolled in college, they had similar two-year persistence rates to never English Learners, regardless of whether they enrolled in a two- or four-year college.

- 47% of ever English Learners who enrolled in two-year colleges persisted for two years, compared to 41% of their never English Learners peers.

- Two-year college persistence was higher for all students who enrolled in four-year colleges. 73% of ever English Learners enrolled in four-year colleges persisted for two years, while 68% of never English Learners did so.

  - Students who persist through the first two years of college are more likely to graduate with a degree,[E] so ever English Learners were on a path to graduate from college at a similar rate to their never English Learners' peers. strong step forward in determining which factors are most important for EL success.

C The data comes from the 5Essentials Survey that CPS students take every year. Students answered the following question: What is the highest level of education you plan to complete? With possible answers being: 1) Not planning to complete high school, 2) High school, 3) Career/technical school, 4) 2-year community college or junior college, 5) 4-year college or university, 6) Graduate or professional school, 7) Undecided, or 8) Other.

D Bowen et al. (2009).

E Nagaoka, Lee, Usher, & Seeskin (2021).

FIGURE A

Ever English Learners had very similar outcomes compared to never English Learners while in high school, but ever English Learners were more likely to enroll in two-year colleges

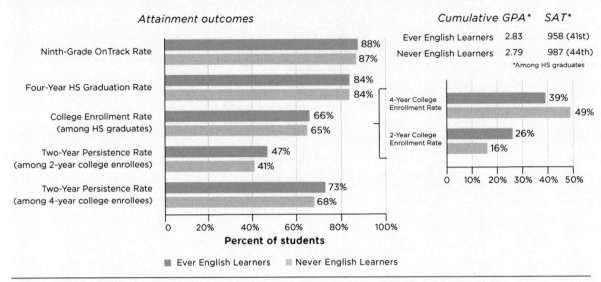

Attainment outcomes

Ninth-Grade OnTrack Rate — 88% / 87%

Four-Year HS Graduation Rate — 84% / 84%

College Enrollment Rate (among HS graduates) — 66% / 65%

Two-Year Persistence Rate (among 2-year college enrollees) — 47% / 41%

Two-Year Persistence Rate (among 4-year college enrollees) — 73% / 68%

Percent of students

	Cumulative GPA*	SAT*
Ever English Learners	2.83	958 (41st)
Never English Learners	2.79	987 (44th)

*Among HS graduates

4-Year College Enrollment Rate — 39% / 49%

2-Year College Enrollment Rate — 26% / 16%

■ Ever English Learners   ■ Never English Learners

Note: The students represented in this graph are students who entered ninth grade for the first time in the fall of 2014, 2015, and 2016.

CHAPTER 4

Implications

The publicly available information on English Learners' performance, focused on active English Learners, suggest that English Learners are a struggling group of students, especially those in high schools. Many researchers have pushed for reporting the data differently to offer a true picture of the performance of all English Learners and to address generalizations and perceptions of English Learners as a homogenous and underperforming group. This study presents metrics on different groups of English Learners to uncover their performance obscured in aggregate numbers and found that, while many former English Learners had strong high school and college outcomes, specific groups of active English Learners need more support throughout high school and college. There are some commonalities among the different groups of English Learners, but also some key differences, suggesting that there should be different strategies for best supporting different types of English Learners. These findings shine a light on where policymakers and educators can focus additional supports.

Long-term English Learners are a group that demands special attention. Over one-quarter of long-term English learner students in our data did not graduate high school in either four or six years, and those who did graduate had lower grades than their peers and were less likely to attend college. These students had been attending CPS schools for six or more years. Their English proficiency test scores were not high enough to be reclassified and continued to be part of the active English Learner category, which qualified them for EL services. But students could be struggling for many reasons and may need support beyond what is needed to pass the English proficiency test. For example, they might not come to school often, they might fail more classes, and school might be more frustrating. Students might be dealing with other challenges that prevent them from engaging in school. One-half of the long-term English Learners had IEPs and nearly all qualified for

free or reduced-price lunch. It is important to understand how they are experiencing school, even before they reach high school, and in what ways they are struggling.

The needs of long-term English Learners without IEPs may not be recognized. Long-term English Learners without IEPs seemed to need help transitioning to high school, as well as more support throughout high school. They were less likely to be on-track in ninth grade, which means they failed some of their classes, and they seemed less likely to get support in ninth grade than long-term English Learners with IEPs who had higher Freshman OnTrack rates.

All students with IEPs need more supports in high school and college. Long-term English Learners with IEPs had similar struggles to other students with IEPs. They seemed to get sufficient support in ninth grade, given their similar Freshman OnTrack rates to district averages, but then fell behind in the following years, with lower high school graduation rates. This suggests the need for more support for all students with IEPs that continues through all four years of high school. They are also likely to need special support for choosing colleges that have strong resources for students with disabilities; their persistence rates were lower than district averages.

Standardized test scores are not good indicators of the potential of late-arriving English Learners, who likely need support around the college enrollment process. Late-arriving English Learners struggled with standardized tests in English because they were still learning English while in high school, but their grades were as strong as or stronger than other students and they were just as likely to graduate high school as students who were never English Learners. Where many need more support is around the college enrollment process—late-arriving English Learners were underrepresented in four-year colleges and overrepresented in two-year colleges, despite strong high school GPAs. They had higher persistence rates than never English Learners and former English Learners when they got to college, suggesting their low test scores were not indicative of a lower likelihood of success. But because they have lower test scores, they may face barriers getting admission to some colleges. Their families might also be less familiar with the post-secondary system in the U.S. and feel less comfortable sending students to colleges that are farther away from home, leading to higher rates of enrollment in two-year colleges that are more likely to be closer to home. Understanding whether late-arriving English Learners faced barriers to enrolling in their desired colleges and what those barriers are would be a starting point to helping them attain college degrees. This is particularly important at this moment, as Chicago and many other cities across the country have seen an increase in the number of English Learners new to the district.

Improving college completion for English Learners includes improving overall completion rates in two-year colleges. All students who were ever English Learners were more likely to enroll in two-year colleges than other students. There is a need to understand how the choices students are making to go to two-year colleges instead of four-year colleges influence their long-term educational attainment and careers. Two-year colleges provide low-cost, local opportunities for college, and more flexible schedules that allow students to work while in college. However, completion rates are lower in two-year colleges. Getting completion rates up in two-year colleges is important for equity, especially for ever English Learners who were more likely to attend these colleges than other students.

We have presented evidence to address the perception that English Learners struggle forever and showed that most students who were or are classified as English Learners are successful, with 84% graduating high school and 66% enrolling in college. Continuously reporting only on active English Learners and the gaps in test scores on tests given in English obscures the successes of English Learners as a group. At the same time, not recognizing the heterogeneity in this group does not allow us to identify that specific groups of English Learners need more support. This study shines a light on what those areas of need are.

References

Allensworth, E., & Easton, J.Q. (2005)
The on-track indicator as a predictor of high school gradu-ation. Chicago, IL: University of Chicago Consortium on Chicago School Research.

Allensworth, E., & Clark, K. (2020)
High school GPAs and ACT scores as predictors of college completion: Examining assumptions about consistency across high schools. *Educational Researcher, 49*(3), 198-211.

Bowen, W.G., Chingos, M.M., & McPherson, M. (2009)
Crossing the finish line. In *Crossing the Finish Line.* Princeton, NJ: Princeton University Press.

Chicago Public Schools. (2024a)
Cohort graduation and dropout rates, 2020 method [Data set]. https://www.cps.edu/about/district-data/metrics/

Chicago Public Schools. (2024b)
College enrollment and persistence data [Data set]. https://www.cps.edu/about/district-data/metrics/

Cohen J. (1988)
Statistical power analysis for the behavioral sciences. New York, NY: Routledge Academic.

College Board. (2023)
Understanding SAT school day scores for students and families. Retrieved from https://satsuite.collegeboard.org/media/pdf/understanding-sat-scores.pdf

Cutler, D.M., & Lleras-Muney, A. (2006)
Education and health: Evaluating theories and evidence (NBER Working Paper No. 12352). Cambridge, MA: National Bureau of Economic Research. Retrieved from http://www.nber.org/papers/w12352

de la Torre, M., Blanchard, A., Allensworth, E.M., & Freire, S. (2019)
English Learners in CPS: A new perspective. Chicago, IL: University of Chicago Consortium on School Research.

Healey, K., Nagaoka, J., & Michelman, V. (2014)
The educational attainment of Chicago Public Schools students: A focus on four-year college degrees. Chicago, IL: University of Chicago Consortium on Chicago School Research.

Mahaffie, S., Usher, A., Nagaoka, J., & McKoy, D. (2024)
The educational attainment of Chicago Public Schools students: 2023. Chicago, IL: University of Chicago Consortium on School Research.

Moretti, E. (2007)
Crime and the costs of criminal justice. In C.R. Belfield & H.M. Levin (Eds.), *The price we pay: Economic and social consequences of inadequate education* (pp. 142–159). Washington, DC: Brookings Institution Press.

Nagaoka, J., Lee, J.S., Usher, A., & Seeskin, A. (2021)
Navigating the maze: Understanding CPS graduates' paths through college. Chicago, IL: University of Chicago Consortium on School Research.

Olsen, L. (2010)
Reparable harm: Fulfilling the unkept promise of educational opportunity for California's long term English Learners. Long Beach, CA: Californians Together.

Roderick, M., Nagaoka, J., Allensworth, E., Coca, V., Correa, M., & Stoker, G. (2006)
From high school to the future: A first look at Chicago Public School graduates' college enrollment, college preparation, and graduation from four-year colleges. Chicago, IL: University of Chicago Consortium on Chicago School Research.

Rouse, C.E. (2007)
Consequences for the labor market. In C.R. Belfield & H.M. Levin (Eds.), *The price we pay: Economic and social consequences of inadequate education* (pp. 99–124). Washington, DC: Brookings Institution Press.

Umansky, I.M. (2016)
Leveled and exclusionary tracking: English Learners' access to academic content in middle school. *American Educational Research Journal, 53*(6), 1792-1833.

Appendix
Analytic Sample and Outcomes

The analytic sample is based on three cohorts of students who started ninth grade for the first time in the fall of 2014, 2015, and 2016, with a total of 78,507 students. These students would have graduated high school in the spring of 2018, 2019, and 2020, respectively. Students were not part of the analytic sample if they enrolled for fewer than 110 days during their ninth-grade year or if their attendance data was not available for that year. This ensures that students were enrolled in CPS schools long enough to take the ACCESS test, which is typically taken in January. This test is required for students classified as English Learners and it helps us define who is an English Learner.

The focus of this report is on the following outcomes: Freshman OnTrack, four-year high school graduation rates, cumulative high school GPA until time of graduation, SAT scores in eleventh grade among high school graduates, immediate college enrollment in any college, two-year and four-year college enrollment among college enrollees, and two-year college persistence rates among two and four-year college enrollees. The number of students included in each outcome varies as follows:

- The Freshman OnTrack rate is based on 76,064 students who did not transfer out from CPS by the end of ninth grade and had on-track data available. A student is on-track if they fail no more than one semester of a core course and earn at least five credits by the end of their ninth-grade year.

- The four-year high school graduation rate is based on 71,290 students who did not transfer out of CPS during the four years since started ninth grade.

- Cumulative high school GPA until time of graduation is based on 46,219 students who graduated high school within four years. Cumulative high school GPA is the average GPA of all the courses a student took from the beginning of high school to the time of graduation.

Students who attended a charter school are not included as our data archive currently does not include records of charter school students' course performance.

- Composite SAT scores are based on 57,853 students who graduated high school within four years and took the SAT in eleventh grade. Composite SAT scores are the average of two assessments, the evidence-based reading and writing section and the math section.

- Immediate college enrollment rates (overall, and in two-year and four-year colleges) are based on 59,737 students who graduated high school within four years and enrolled in the summer or fall after high school graduation. Students are counted toward the two-year college enrollment rate if they enrolled in a two-year college in that time frame and are counted toward the four-year college enrollment rate if they enrolled in a four-year college in that time frame.

- The two-year college persistence rate is based on students who immediately enrolled in college. A student is considered to have persisted in college for two years if they were enrolled in college for at least two years, with records in four consecutive fall and spring terms, or attained an associate degree or bachelor's degree, within six years of starting ninth grade. In particular,
    - the two-year persistence rate among two-year college enrollees is based on 12,041 students who graduated high school within four years and immediately enrolled in a two-year college, and
    - the two-year persistence rate among four-year college enrollees is based on 27,555 students who graduated high school within four years and immediately enrolled in a four-year college.

Methods

The graphs presented in this report are based on simple averages of the outcomes for the different groups of English Learners. However, English Learners in CPS are more likely to be eligible for free or reduced-price lunch and to be Latinx. In some subgroups, English Learners were more likely to be male or to have an IEP. For this reason, it is important to analyze the outcomes taking into account these characteristics to uncover whether some of these characteristics increase, decrease or do not affect the results observed in the raw data.

The following tables present the results of regressions for each outcome, controlling for some student characteristics. The outcomes and the variables included in the models, with the exception of the dummy variables representing never English Learner, former English Learner, long-term English Learner no IEP, long-term English Learner with IEP, and late-arriving English Learner, have been transformed by subtracting their overall mean so the estimates for each student group from these regressions represent differences with respect to the district average. The first column reflects the results from a linear model with a series of dummy variables representing the different groups of students with no controls and therefore represents the differences depicted in the graphs (because of rounding issues the values might not be exactly the same). For example in **Table A.1**, the Freshman OnTrack rate for never English Learners is 0.2 percentage points below the district average (87.3% for never English Learners and 87.5% for district average) and for former English Learners is 2.5 percentage points above the district average (90.0% for former English Learners vs. 87.5% for the district average). Figure 2 in the main text shows these numbers rounded.

The next column (2) presents the results of a linear model adding a series of dummy variables representing different IEP categories. The last column (3) contains the results from a model with variables representing IEP categories, free or reduced-price lunch eligibility (FRPL), race/ethnicity, and gender together and can be interpreted as the differences among groups of students if the groups were similar in terms of all these variables.

Although many of the estimates are statistically significant, we describe outcomes as being substantially or meaningfully different among groups of students when the difference is 0.2 standard deviations or higher. Differences that are larger than 0.2 standard deviations are in the shaded cells. We also mention in the main part of the report when differences in outcomes become larger or smaller than 0.2 standard deviations when comparing similar students. For example, in **Table A.2,** the differences in high school graduation rates are substantial (more than 0.2 standard deviations) for long-term English Learners with IEP, however, the differences become smaller than 0.2 standard deviations when compared to other students with IEPs.

Estimates for Freshman OnTrack (percentage points differences from district average)

	No Other Variables (1)	IEP (2)	All Variables: IEP, FRPL, race/ethnicity, and gender (3)
Never English Learners	-0.2	-0.2	-0.0
Former English Learners	2.5***	2.2***	2.1***
Long-term English Learners no IEP	-10.8***	-11.3***	-10.4***
Long-term English Learners with IEP	-1.1+	1.3+	0.5
Late-arriving English Learners	-0.2	-0.5	-2.2**
Number of Observations	76,064	76,064	76,064
R-squared	0.006	0.013	0.038

Note: + p<0.10, * p<0.05, ** p<0.01, *** p<0.001. Shaded cells (blue) represent differences larger than 0.2 standard deviations.

TABLE A.2

Estimates for four-year high school graduation (percentage points differences from district average)

	No Other Variables (1)	IEP (2)	All Variables: IEP, FRPL, race/ethnicity, and gender (3)
Never English Learners	0.0	0.2	0.1
Former English Learners	4.0***	2.4***	2.7***
Long-term English Learners no IEP	-10.1***	-12.4***	-11.1***
Long-term English Learners with IEP	-15.1***	-3.3***	-3.8***
Late-arriving English Learners	-3.2***	-4.4***	-5.9***
Number of Observations	71,290	71,290	71,290
R-squared	0.012	0.051	0.073

Note: + p<0.10, * p<0.05, ** p<0.01, *** p<0.001. Shaded cells (blue) represent differences larger than 0.2 standard deviations.

TABLE A.3

Estimates for cumulative GPA among high school graduates (GPA points differences from district average)

	No Other Variables (1)	IEP (2)	All Variables: IEP, FRPL, race/ethnicity, and gender (3)
Never English Learners	-0.01**	-0.02***	-0.02***
Former English Learners	0.09***	0.06***	0.01*
Long-term English Learners no IEP	-0.31***	-0.36***	-0.35***
Long-term English Learners with IEP	-0.26***	0.08**	-0.01
Late-arriving English Learners	0.06**	0.04+	-0.12***
Number of Observations	46,219	46,219	46,219
R-squared	0.014	0.039	0.209

Note: + p<0.10, * p<0.05, ** p<0.01, *** p<0.001. Shaded cells (blue) represent differences larger than 0.2 standard deviations.

Estimates for composite SAT among high school graduates (SAT points differences from district average)

	No Other Variables (1)	IEP (2)	All Variables: IEP, FRPL, race/ethnicity, and gender (3)
Never English Learners	9.7***	9.0***	17.6***
Former English Learners	26.2***	9.9***	-8.4***
Long-term English Learners no IEP	-139.4***	-164.9***	-165.1***
Long-term English Learners with IEP	-206.1***	-19.3***	-54.6***
Late-arriving English Learners	-95.3***	-109.3***	-160.6***
Number of Observations	57,853	57,853	57,853
R-squared	0.065	0.162	0.388

Note: + p<0.10, * p<0.05, ** p<0.01, *** p<0.001. Shaded cells (blue) represent differences larger than 0.2 standard deviations.

TABLE A.5

Estimates for immediate college enrollment among high school graduates (percentage points differences from district average)

	No Other Variables (1)	IEP (2)	All Variables: IEP, FRPL, race/ethnicity, and gender (3)
Never English Learners	-0.2	-0.2	0.8**
Former English Learners	4.7***	2.9***	1.2**
Long-term English Learners no IEP	-10.97***	-13.8***	-13.9***
Long-term English Learners with IEP	-21.0***	-0.3	-3.7**
Late-arriving English Learners	-3.9**	-5.5***	-9.6***
Number of Observations	59,737	59,737	59,737
R-squared	0.010	0.031	0.068

Note: + p<0.10, * p<0.05, ** p<0.01, *** p<0.001. Shaded cells (blue) represent differences larger than 0.2 standard deviations.

TABLE A.6

Estimates for immediate college enrollment in two-year colleges among high school graduates (percentage points differences from district average)

	No Other Variables (1)	IEP (2)	All Variables: IEP, FRPL, race/ethnicity, and gender (3)
Never English Learners	-3.4***	-3.4***	-1.5***
Former English Learners	5.6***	5.8***	2.1***
Long-term English Learners no IEP	11.8***	12.2***	7.5***
Long-term English Learners with IEP	8.1***	5.3***	0.5
Late-arriving English Learners	9.2***	9.4***	9.0***
Number of Observations	59,737	59,737	59,737
R-squared	0.016	0.016	0.029

Note: + p<0.10, * p<0.05, ** p<0.01, *** p<0.001. Shaded cells (blue) represent differences larger than 0.2 standard deviations.

Estimates for immediate college enrollment in four-year colleges among high school graduates
(percentage points differences from district average)

	No Other Variables (1)	IEP (2)	All Variables: IEP, FRPL, race/ethnicity, and gender (3)
Never English Learners	3.3***	3.3***	2.3***
Former English Learners	-1.0*	-2.9***	-0.9*
Long-term English Learners no IEP	-22.7***	-26.0***	-21.4***
Long-term English Learners with IEP	-29.1***	-5.6***	-4.1**
Late-arriving English Learners	-13.1***	-14.9***	-18.6***
Number of Observations	59,737	59,737	59,737
R-squared	0.022	0.045	0.088

Note: + $p<0.10$, * $p<0.05$, ** $p<0.01$, *** $p<0.001$. Shaded cells (blue) represent differences larger than 0.2 standard deviations.

Estimates for two-year persistence in college among enrollees in two-year colleges (percentage points differences from district average)

	No Other Variables (1)	IEP (2)	All Variables: IEP, FRPL, race/ethnicity, and gender (3)
Never English Learners	-2.5***	-2.5***	-0.5
Former English Learners	5.0***	4.3***	2.3*
Long-term English Learners no IEP	-3.6+	-4.8*	-6.4**
Long-term English Learners with IEP	-4.8*	2.6	-0.9
Late-arriving English Learners	4.1+	3.3	-2.6
Number of Observations	12,041	12,041	12,041
R-squared	0.006	0.009	0.052

Note: + $p<0.10$, * $p<0.05$, ** $p<0.01$, *** $p<0.001$. Shaded cells (blue) represent differences larger than 0.2 standard deviations.

Estimates for two-year persistence in college among enrollees in four-year colleges (percentage points differences from district average)

	No Other Variables (1)	IEP (2)	All Variables: IEP, FRPL, race/ethnicity, and gender (3)
Never English Learners	-1.3***	-1.3***	-0.7*
Former English Learners	4.2***	3.7***	2.2**
Long-term English Learners no IEP	-6.4**	-7.4**	-5.9*
Long-term English Learners with IEP	-13.1***	2.2	-1.2
Late-arriving English Learners	8.5***	8.0***	3.9*
Number of Observations	27,555	27,555	27,555
R-squared	0.005	0.011	0.084

Note: + $p<0.10$, * $p<0.05$, ** $p<0.01$, *** $p<0.001$. Shaded cells (blue) represent differences larger than 0.2 standard deviations.

ABOUT THE AUTHORS

MARISA DE LA TORRE is a Senior Research Associate and Managing Director at the UChicago Consortium. Her research interests include urban school reform, school choice, early indicators of school success, and English Learners. Before joining the UChicago Consortium, Marisa worked for the Chicago Public Schools in the Office of Research, Evaluation, and Accountability. She received a master's degree in economics from Northwestern University.

ALYSSA BLANCHARD is a Research Associate in WestEd's Economic Mobility, Postsecondary, and Workforce Systems Content Area. Her current work includes an evaluation of Clemson University's Teacher Quality Partnership, a teacher preparation program in rural South Carolina. She is also working on an evaluation of the City Colleges of Chicago's Chancellor's Retention Grant and Working Credit program, which is aimed at increasing student retention of community college students. Prior to her work at WestEd, Blanchard conducted research on educator pipelines and English Learners at the UChicago Consortium. She received an MPP in educational policy and a BA in public policy from Vanderbilt University.

KAITLYN FRANKLIN is a Research Analyst at the UChicago Consortium, providing data and analytic support across Consortium projects by cleaning and building large-scale databases. She is currently working to identify key indicators of student success and academic attainment for English Learners in Chicago Public Schools. Before joining the UChicago Consortium, Kaitlyn served as the Education Policy Intern for Clarke County School District in Athens, Georgia. There, she designed, wrote, and implemented monthly policy briefings and overhauled the district's policy organization system to streamline the policy review process. Kaitlyn is passionate about working toward more equitable opportunities and outcomes for students in the public school system.

CARLOS L. ANGELES is an Institute of Education Sciences Fellow and doctoral student at the University of Chicago Crown School of Social Work, Policy, and Practice. Carlos's research interests broadly include social and racial inequality within urban education, prek-12 education reform, and the politics of the teaching profession. Using a mix of qualitative and quantitative methods, Carlos is investigating policies and practices that address educational inequality for students of color, immigrant, and Latinx students. Carlos served as an educator and administrator in Chicago and New York City schools and has extensive teaching experience.

ELAINE M. ALLENSWORTH is the Lewis-Sebring Director of the University of Chicago Consortium on Chicago School Research, where she has conducted research on educational policy and practice for over 25 years. Her research examines factors influencing students' educational attainment, school leadership, and school improvement. She works with policymakers and practitioners to bridge research and practice, serving on panels, policy commissions, and working groups at the local, state and national levels.

Made in the USA
Monee, IL
22 February 2025

11987418R00024